CW01560609

Homemade Chocolate:
The Kickstart Guide to Making Delicious Chocolates

Homemade Chocolate:
The Kickstart Guide to Making Delicious Chocolates
by **Lynne Parcell**

Printed in the United States of America

Copyright © 2012 **Lynne Parcell**

Disclaimer

Legal Notice:- The author and publisher of this Ebook and the accompanying materials have used their best efforts in preparing this Ebook. The author and publisher make no representation or warranties with respect to the accuracy, applicability, fitness, or completeness of the contents of this Ebook. The information contained in this Ebook is strictly for educational purposes. Therefore, if you wish to apply ideas contained in this Ebook, you are taking full responsibility for your actions.

The author and publisher disclaim any warranties (express or implied), merchantability, or fitness for any particular purpose. The author and publisher shall in no event be held liable to any party for any direct, indirect, punitive, special, incidental or other consequential damages arising directly or indirectly from any use of this material, which is provided "as is", and without warranties.

As always, the advice of a competent legal, tax, accounting or other professional should be sought. The author and publisher do not warrant the performance, effectiveness or applicability of any sites listed or linked to in this Ebook. All links are for information purposes only and are not warranted for content, accuracy or any other implied or explicit purpose.

Table of Contents

Chapter 1

Why Should You Make
Homemade Chocolate

Homemade Chocolate: The Kickstart Guide on Making Delicious Chocolates

Most people have never really even though about making their own homemade chocolate, they just buy chocolate bars or chocolate cookies at the store and don't think twice about it. But people have been making homemade chocolate for hundreds of years. Some people think that homemade chocolate tastes much better than commercial chocolate. And who doesn't love getting a special chocolate treat that was made just for them?

For people that have special medical conditions or dietary challenges that make it unhealthy for them to eat commercial chocolate that is loaded with sugar and fat making homemade chocolate is a good way for them to be able to enjoy having some chocolate without having to worry about the health problems that they would face from eating commercially made chocolate.

People that have severe allergies to things that are often found in commercially made chocolate, like nuts, have to be extremely careful about the types and brands of commercially made chocolate that they eat and many prefer to make homemade chocolate so that they know it's free of any nuts or nut products.

This is a huge concern for people that have diabetes because chocolate can wreak havoc with a diabetic's blood sugar levels. Many doctors recommend that people who suffer from Diabetes give up chocolate all together or only eat sugar free chocolate. Since it can be hard to find sugar free chocolate that is tasty and not expensive making homemade sugar free chocolate is a great alternative for diabetics. If you have a diabetic family member you can make that person feel more at home on holidays or at parties by making special homemade sugar free chocolate that they can eat.

Another reason that you should give homemade chocolate making a try is because it's fun. If you enjoy cooking then you will probably really enjoy the creative process of deciding what type of chocolates to make, the experience of actually making the chocolate, and then of course comes the fun of eating the chocolate. Making homemade chocolate is a great rainy day activity that you can do with the kids to keep them busy and the chocolates that you make are wonderful

Homemade Chocolate: The Kickstart Guide on Making Delicious Chocolates

gifts and party favors for holidays, birthdays, and other occasions.

Making homemade chocolate can also be a lot less expensive than buying commercially made chocolates, especially around holidays like Christmas or Valentine's Day. If you want to have some great gifts that people will really love without spending a fortune then you can make homemade chocolate gifts for people that are unique and personalized and don't cost that much to make. Most people love to get homemade gifts and almost everyone loves chocolate so giving the gift of homemade chocolate is sure to be a hit.

Chapter 2

Traditional Chocolate Making

Homemade Chocolate: The Kickstart Guide on Making Delicious Chocolates

Making chocolate the traditional way can be done at home, although it's a lengthy and involved process. If you want to pursue making homemade chocolate as a hobby and it's important to you to make all of your chocolate from scratch you can do that but you'll need some specialized equipment and a lot of time on your hands. Some people really do enjoy making chocolate from scratch, so you should give traditional chocolate making a try to see if it's a hobby that you are interested in pursuing. Using a traditional process to make chocolate home has several steps:

• Choosing the beans. Chocolate is made from cacao beans so when you first start off making chocolate the traditional way you need to start with some high quality cacao beans. There are suppliers on the Internet that sell different varieties of cacao beans in many different price ranges so if you are looking for whole cacao beans it isn't too hard to find them.

• Roasting the beans. Cacao beans need to be roasted just like coffee beans. You can roast them at home on a cookie sheet in the oven if you watch them carefully or you can buy a specialized cacao bean roaster for at home use if you're going

Homemade Chocolate: The Kickstart Guide on Making Delicious Chocolates

to pursue traditional candy making as a hobby. The beans are usually roasted for as little as five minutes or as many as 35 minutes depending on the type of bean and the flavor that you want to achieve.

• Getting the chocolate out. After the beans are roasted you need to crack open the outer shell of the bean to get the chocolate that is inside out. There are several ways to do this at home. You can lay the beans in a single sheet on a counter or on a baking sheet and use a hammer to crack the shells open, then use a blow dryer on a low setting to blow the hulls of the beans away from the chocolate or you can use a juicer to accomplish the same goal. This step can be very messy, so make sure that you have a mop and bucket and lots of clean up supplies standing by.

• Grinding and Refining the chocolate. Now you need to grind the chocolate down as fine as possible. If you're going to do this at home many expert chocolate makers recommend using a high quality juicer to grind the chocolate. After the chocolate has all been ground as finely as possible you need to add milk, sugar, preservatives, or anything else that you're planning on adding to the chocolate to enhance the flavor. Once everything is mixed with the other ingredients the chocolate will need to be agitated slowly but constantly. This process could take up to 12 hours to get the chocolate to exactly the right consistency. Experts recommend using a stand mixer on a low setting to refine the chocolate.

•   Tempering the chocolate. Once the chocolate has been fully refined it needs to be tempered before you can use it. Tempering chocolate at home can be a very complicated process but if you want to cheat a little and speed up the procedure you can use a microwave to temper your homemade chocolate. Once the chocolate is tempered and is smooth, hard and shiny it's ready to be used or eaten.

Making Chocolate

Ever wonder how chocolate is made? The short story is that these are made from bitter cacao beans and then molded into chocolate bars. If you were a chocolate company like Hershey's, you would need a lot of them and to give you an idea

Homemade Chocolate: The Kickstart Guide on Making Delicious Chocolates

how it is made, here is a guide in the production process.

The first thing that needs to be done is to harvest the cacao beans. Large companies buy these from farmers or buy the farm and harvest these themselves. They then put these in an oven at a temperature between 120 to 163 degrees Celsius that is about 250 to 325 degrees Fahrenheit for 5 to 35 minutes.

Naturally, you will gradually lower the temperature and stop roasting them when the beans start to crack.

There are two reasons why cacao beans stay in an oven at varying times.

First is to prevent them from burning. Naturally, you will gradually lower the temperature and stop roasting them when the beans start to crack. Naturally, you will gradually lower the temperature and stop roasting them when the beans start to crack.

Second, the cooking time of cacao beans varies

Homemade Chocolate: The Kickstart Guide on Making Delicious Chocolates

depending on the type of bean that is being used.

Since companies produce chocolates in vast quantities, the cacao beans are stored in drums and then rotated over a gas grill. After they are roasted, the beans must be cracked into small bits better known as nibs while those that can't are removed.

The next step is to grind the nibs into a cacao liqueur. For that, you will need a machine to liquefy this and at the same time separate the remaining husks that were not removed after roasting.

You then conch and refine the chocolate so you are able to give the chocolate its distinct taste. This is what makes Hershey's chocolates different than for example M&M which can be achieved by using a powerful wet grinder.

You first have to melt the chocolate and the cocoa butter in the over at about 120 degrees Fahrenheit. You should then mix non fat dry milk powder, sugar, lecithin and a vanilla pod for about an hour. This mixture is then poured into a grinder

Homemade Chocolate: The Kickstart Guide on Making Delicious Chocolates

together with some heat to keep the chocolate in liquid form. This should be refined for at least 10 hours but not more than 36 hours.

When it is ready, you then temper the chocolate so it looks shiny and soft enough to easily melt in your hand.

The second to the last part in making chocolate is to mold this into whatever shape or form that you would like. To produce these in vast quantities, chocolate companies but custom made molds. The chocolate is then poured there and after this is cooled, this is then packaged and ready for delivery to stores.

Some companies even sell these in the form of blocks so people can buy them, melt it and mold this to whatever shape they desire.

Making chocolate is easy as long as you have the equipment and all the ingredients needed. It doesn't matter if this is produced in large volumes or in small quantities because the principle behind it is the same. If you want to learn more about making chocolate, sign up for some classes.

Chapter 3

Making Great Homemade
Chocolate Without a Lot of Work

Homemade Chocolate: The Kickstart Guide on Making Delicious Chocolates

Does the process of making chocolate in a tradition way seem like a lot of hard work that you don't really want to do? Some people love the lengthy process of making chocolate in a traditional fashion but some people want a faster, easier way to get homemade chocolate. For those people, deciding what to use to flavor the chocolate and using unique molds is the fun part of making homemade chocolate.

To make it easier to get to the fun part of homemade chocolate making you can skip the traditional chocolate making process and use special chocolate chips and wafers that are made for candy making. These chips and wafers are great because you can melt them down in a double boiler or even in a microwave and then you have a great smooth chocolate base to start with and you can get creative deciding what to add to the chocolate to make it uniquely yours.

When you use these chips, wafers and bricks of chocolate to make your own chocolate you'll be amazed at how creative you can. For many people the traditional way of making chocolate is far too difficult and time consuming. Most people

Homemade Chocolate: The Kickstart Guide on Making Delicious Chocolates

just want to be able to make up some cool homemade treats in their kitchen, they don't want to have to do a lot of research or find special ingredients or invest in a lot of pricey equipment just make some chocolate at home.

If you're one of those people that wants to get right to the fun part of making chocolate at home, mixing the chocolates and coming up with new chocolate recipes and so on then you should definitely buy some chocolate base from a candy supply shop or a craft store and start to make your own candy using those melt and pour chocolates.

Using melt and pour chocolate is also a great way to try out different chocolate flavors. You can get some very exotic chocolate bases that are full of special spices that would cost a fortune if you wanted to buy individually and add to your chocolate. You can also get sugar free and low fat chocolate bases that eliminate the need for you to buy pricey ingredients or measure ingredients to make chocolate that is sugar free or low fat.

If you want to have a lot of fun making homemade chocolate, save some money and make great gifts

Homemade Chocolate: The Kickstart Guide on Making Delicious Chocolates

that all your friends will love then making chocolate using some great melt and pour chocolate bases will be perfect for you.

Look in your local craft store to see if they carry candy making supplies or look online to find a candy supply store that carries a wide selection of different chocolates that you can use to make homemade chocolate.

Chapter 4

Best Types of Chocolate to Use in Homemade Chocolate

Homemade Chocolate: The Kickstart Guide on Making Delicious Chocolates

When it comes to making your own homemade chocolate there are lots of different chocolates that can use depending on your tastes and who you are making the chocolate for. For example, dark chocolate has no milk products in it so if you are making chocolate for someone that is a vegan or someone that is lactose intolerant you should use a dark chocolate base because it doesn't contain any milk. Here is a quick overview of the most common types of chocolate that you can use to make your own homemade chocolate:

Unsweetened chocolate – You probably have has some experience with unsweetened chocolate before. Unsweetened chocolate is often used in baking to add a rich chocolate flavor to food. You can unsweetened chocolate as a base to make sugar free chocolate and use something other than sugar to give the chocolate a sweeter taste. Many people that are diabetic or are watching their sugar intake will use unsweetened chocolate and a sugar substitute to make their own homemade chocolate.

•   Dark chocolate – As previously stated, dark chocolate has no milk in it so it's great to use as a

Homemade Chocolate: The Kickstart Guide on Making Delicious Chocolates

base for people that can't or choose not to eat milk or milk products. Some people also enjoy the dark, slightly bitter taste of dark chocolate.

•　　　Bittersweet chocolate – This chocolate is slightly sweeter than unsweetened chocolate that has no sugar in it at all but it has very little sugar in it. If you want to make chocolate that has a lot less sugar than other types of chocolate but you don't want to use a commercial sugar substitute you can use bittersweet chocolate as a base for your homemade chocolates.

•　　　Semi-sweet chocolate – Semi-sweet chocolate is slightly sweeter than bittersweet chocolate and has a slightly higher sugar content but still has a lower sugar content than most chocolate. Semi-sweet is one of the most popular type of chocolates used in candy making and is also often used in making chocolate chip cookies.

•　　　Milk chocolate – Milk chocolate is a rich chocolate that contains high levels of sugar and at least 12% milk or milk solids. Most milk chocolate is made with condensed or evaporated milk. Milk chocolate is very sweet and has a very low cocoa

Homemade Chocolate: The Kickstart Guide on Making Delicious Chocolates

content so it doesn't have the bitter or slightly harsh taste that other chocolates have.

• White Chocolate – White chocolate is really not chocolate, it's a confection made of cocoa butter, sugar and milk that is often flavored with vanilla or other flavors. It's called chocolate because it contains cocoa butter but there is no actual cocoa in it.

You can always experiment with different flavors by mixing and matching different types of chocolate too. For example, a touch of milk chocolate might give your semi-sweet homemade chocolate a little bit of richness that will really enhance the flavor. Play around with the different kinds of chocolate until you find a mixture that really tastes great and make that your "signature" chocolate base.

Chapter 5

5 Tools You Will Need to Make Homemade Chocolate

Homemade Chocolate: The Kickstart Guide on Making Delicious Chocolates

Some books and magazines about candy making will say that you need to have a lot of special equipment in order to make chocolate at home but that's not necessarily true. There are really only five tools that you have to have in order to make great chocolate at home and you probably already have at least some of them in your kitchen. They are:

•   Candy thermometer – Some chocolate candy does need to be heated to a certain temperature in order to be safe to eat, and some types of chocolate need to be heated to a certain temperature in order to be liquid enough to pour and set properly in a mold so it's a good idea to have at least one candy thermometer on hand.

•   Mixing bowls – You will go through mixing bowls like crazy when you are making chocolate, especially if you are mixing other ingredients into a chocolate base. To save money on mixing bowls go to your local Goodwill or Salvation Army store. Charity shops like that usually have kitchen and house wares sections where you can find great deals on glass and stainless steel mixing bowls. You can also look for mixing bowls at garage and yard sales.

• Pots and pans -If you are using pre-made chocolate base you can heat that base in a microwave until it's liquid enough to work with but you will need saucepans to mix in other ingredients and bring the chocolate to the correct temperature. Just like mixing bowls you can often find mismatched pots and pans at charity stores and garage sales. You can also use two pans to make your own double boiler when a chocolate recipe calls for you to use a double boiler.

• Molds – Once you have your chocolate blended just the way you want it and have added any extras that you want to add into the chocolate you're going to need something to pour that chocolate into so that you can make chocolate candies. It's always good idea to have a wide variety of chocolate molds that are clean and ready to go.

• Candy Coloring – If you want to really decorate your handmade chocolates and make them fun shapes and colors you will need to use special candy coloring. Normal food coloring won't

Homemade Chocolate: The Kickstart Guide on Making Delicious Chocolates

color chocolate. To get the colors to show on the chocolate it's necessary to have special food coloring that is made for candy and chocolate. You can find candy coloring at any craft supply store or candy supply store.

These are just a few of the supplies that you might need to make chocolate but if you have these supplies always on hand then you shouldn't have any trouble making delicious homemade chocolates at any time. If you are going to make a special type of chocolate or you want to use a special recipe then you might need specialized equipment but in general you can get by just using these pieces of equipment and what you already have in your kitchen.

Chapter 6

Making Sugar Free Chocolate

Homemade Chocolate: The Kickstart Guide on Making Delicious Chocolates

If you or a loved one is Diabetic or is on a diet where they can't tolerate sugar making your own sugar free chocolate is a great way that you or they can enjoy a sweet treat without sugar. If you are making desserts for a party or dinner and have friends or family attending it would be a thoughtful gesture to include some sugar free chocolates on the menu so that the people who can't have sugar or are watching their sugar intake could still have a nice dessert.

There are several ways that you can make your own sugar free chocolate. If you are handy in the kitchen and feel comfortable making your own chocolate you can use a base chocolate like unsweetened chocolate that has no sugar in it but you'll have to add something to the chocolate to make it sweet. If you can use a sugar substitute that has the same consistency that sugar has that is probably the best route but you can also add things like fruit juice to the unsweetened chocolate to sweeten it.

When you are combining unsweetened chocolate with a sugar substitute you should always mix the two ingredients when they are dry, otherwise they won't combine properly and they will separate when they are wet. If you are using fruit juice to sweeten the unsweetened chocolate pour in very small amounts and make sure that you add a thickener to the chocolate to keep the chocolate at the right consistency.

If you don't feel comfortable trying to take an unsweetened chocolate base and trying to sweeten it yourself you can always buy sugar free or diabetic friendly chocolate in blocks or in chips from candy supply houses and then use that as a base for your chocolate treats. Most candy supply houses carry a range of sugar free chocolates including dark chocolate and milk chocolate that is all made with a sugar substitute so that it's safe for anyone that can't eat sugar to eat.

Once you have an unsweetened or sugar free chocolate base you can make chocolate candy the same way that you would with regular chocolate by pouring it into molds and letting the candy harden. But if you want to make a fancy chocolate dessert like a chocolate mousse, or a chocolate dipping sauce for fresh fruit, or even sugar free hot chocolate you can still use the sugar free

Homemade Chocolate: The Kickstart Guide on Making Delicious Chocolates

chocolate as a base and then you can experiment with different recipes using the sugar free chocolate as an ingredient.

You can even make sugar free chocolate chip cookies by chopping up small chips of the sugar free chocolate base and adding them to some sugar free cookie dough although you will have to be careful what temperature you bake the cookies at or the chocolate will melt.

If you are planning on making holiday treats or chocolates as gifts for your kid's teachers, friends and neighbors, or anyone that you don't know very well it's always a good idea to include at least a few sugar free chocolates in the gift package because you never know if someone can have chocolate that has regular sugar in it or not. People that can't have sugar will find it very thoughtful that you included some sugar free chocolates in the gift.

Chapter 7

Making Low Fat Chocolate

Homemade Chocolate: The Kickstart Guide on Making Delicious Chocolates

If you are on a diet or if someone in your house is trying to lose weight then you might want to try making some low fat chocolate that you can keep around the house or give to your friends as gifts. Homemade low fat chocolates are very popular as desserts for sleepover parties or as party favors at teen birthday favors. It's also nice to have some low fat chocolates around when you want to be able to enjoy some chocolate without having to worry about how much fat you're eating.

One way to make low fat chocolates at home is to look for some pre-made low fat chocolate chips or bricks that you can melt down and use to make your own candies. But if you can't find low fat chocolate that is pre-made or you don't want to spend a lot of money on a pricey pre-made chocolate base you can easily make your own low fat version of traditional chocolate that you can use to make brownies, cookies, or candy treats. A low fat chocolate dipping sauce for fresh fruit makes a great low fat and low calorie dessert that won't make you feel like you're missing out on treat.

Use these tips to make your own low fat

29

Homemade Chocolate: The Kickstart Guide on Making Delicious Chocolates

chocolate:

• Develop a taste for dark chocolate. Since dark chocolate has no milk products in it dark chocolate hast the lowest fat content of the different kinds of chocolate.

• Substitute bittersweet or semi-sweet chocolate for milk chocolate. The less milk and cocoa butter that the chocolate has the lower the fat content will be

• Don't add extras to your chocolate. If you must add something to the chocolate make it some chopped nuts that are good for your heart or raisins which are healthier and lower in fat then adding things like candy pieces or peanut butter chips.

• Use a chocolate coating instead of chocolate. If you are craving a sweet dessert but really want to keep your fat intake low make a low fat chocolate dipping sauce from some semi-sweet or dark chocolate and then just lightly coat some fresh fruit, a granola bar, or some other low fat, healthy snack with the chocolate. That way

Homemade Chocolate: The Kickstart Guide on Making Delicious Chocolates

you'll still get a chocolate fix but you won't be eating a lot of fat to get it.

•   Make some low fat hot chocolate instead of candy. Make some low fat hot chocolate using dark chocolate and enjoy a warm cup of hot chocolate instead of making brownies or another type of high fat dessert.

•   These are just some simple ways that you can still have chocolate treats without worrying about ruining your diet or going overboard on your fat intake. If you have kids and you're concerned by how much fat your kids eat just substituting some low fat chocolate instead of regular chocolate in cookies, brownies, and chocolate milk can make a big difference in how much fat your kids are eating every day.

Chapter 8

5 Fun Ways to Make Your Chocolate Unique

Homemade Chocolate: The Kickstart Guide on Making Delicious Chocolates

One of the most fun things about making your own homemade chocolate is that you can play around with different ingredients and make your own unique chocolate recipes and chocolate treats. Putting your individual stamp on the chocolate that you make will also make it more personal when you give the chocolate as gifts to people that you love. And if someday you want to go further and actually sell the homemade chocolate that you make then having your own unique chocolates will make it a lot easier to sell your chocolate.

But most people that make homemade chocolate use the same basic types of chocolate and the same base chocolate mixes from candy supply stores so how can you make your own unique chocolates without making your chocolate entirely from scratch? Here are five easy ways that you can create delicious treats that reflect your own personal style:

•	Mix chocolate bases – Just because a lot of people that make homemade chocolate use the same bases doesn't mean that you can't make your base chocolate unique. You can use the same chocolate bases from candy supply stores

Homemade Chocolate: The Kickstart Guide on Making Delicious Chocolates

that other people use but just combine them in a unique way to make your own signature flavor. Mixing dark chocolate and milk chocolate, or semisweet chocolate with white chocolate, or mixing other flavors together to create your own unique base can be a great way to make your homemade chocolates stand out from the crowd.

•   Add things to your base chocolate – There are lots of things that you can add to your chocolate base to make your chocolates tastier and more unique. You can use toasted sesame seeds to provide crunch, or you can use peanut butter, seeds, nuts, fruits, and lots of other things to make chocolates that are different and delicious.

•   Make your own molds – Think outside the box when it comes to the molds that you use to put your chocolates in. Instead of just using traditional candy molds in traditional shapes use cake molds, soap molds, cookie cutters and other tools to make fun and unique shapes for your chocolates. If you want to make your own molds you can find books and the supplies that you need to make your own plastic molds at most craft

Homemade Chocolate: The Kickstart Guide on Making Delicious Chocolates

stores.

• Use unique packages – How you pack your candy can become a signature style for you that will set your chocolate apart from other chocolates and apart from commercial candy too. Instead of using traditional boxes look for fun and unique ways to package your candy like using hand painted box or little cello bags.

• Use decorations – Using candy coloring and other fun decorations on your chocolates can help you turn even the plainest homemade chocolate into a fun treat. Make sure that you package decorated candy properly to make sure that the decorations don't fall off in the package.

Chapter 9

Using Molds

Homemade Chocolate: The Kickstart Guide on Making Delicious Chocolates

Using molds is a great way to make your chocolate fun and interesting. You can use basic molds that are just in traditional shapes like squares or bars or you can use fun molds that are in all different shapes and styles. If you want to make lollipops or suckers there are special molds that you can use to make those.

There are lots of companies that make special candy molds that are specifically made to be used with chocolate. These are often found in holiday shapes like Easter bunnies, chicks, and eggs or in Christmas shapes like Santa Claus, stars, and Christmas trees. There are candy molds out there for every season so you shouldn't have any trouble finding a mold that will be perfect for you holiday celebration.

But you're not limited to just using candy molds for your chocolate. You can use soap molds, cake molds, or other types of molds too. As long as a mold is made from a heavy plastic it should work just fine. To make your candy slide out of the mold more easily spray the inside of the mold with a no stick cooking spray. That way you won't have a situation where half of your chocolate candy ends up stuck inside the mold. If chocolate does get stuck inside a mold turn then mold over so that the open side is facing down and run the mold under the hot water tap until the chocolate loosens and slides out.

To take care of your molds make sure that you wash each one thoroughly after you're done with it. Molds can be washed with normal soap and water like dishes almost most are not dishwasher safe so don't put them in the dishwasher unless the mold says that it's dishwasher safe.

When you pour the chocolate into the molds it might take several hours or even several days for the chocolate to harden in the mold. Even though you might be tempted to put the chocolate and the mold into the freezer so that it hardens more quickly you shouldn't do that. It will make the chocolate harden too fast and it can damage the mold. You can put the chocolate filled mold in the refrigerator though, and that should help the chocolate solidify in the mold more quickly.

Using molds is a cheap and easy way to make your homemade chocolate more fun. Getting your

Homemade Chocolate: The Kickstart Guide on Making Delicious Chocolates

candy out of a mold can be tricky but one way that you can make it easier to get the chocolate out of the mold once it's hard is to drop the mold onto the counter before you set it down to loosen the chocolate inside the mold. Running the mold under a little hot water is also a good way to get chocolate candy out of a mold.

You can find candy and craft molds at any craft store, and sometimes at the grocery store too. Some craft stores carry thin plastic molds that are very cheap but these don't last very long so they're not really a bargain. Spend a few dollars more and get molds made from high density plastic that are very thick. They're really worth the extra cost.

Making Chocolate from Molds

In the late 1800's, chocolate makers already used molds made from metal. This made it possible to shape them either as flat or three dimensional. Plastic soon replaced that as these were expensive to produce making it possible for amateur chocolatiers to make these at home.

Homemade Chocolate: The Kickstart Guide on Making Delicious Chocolates

When you buy chocolate molds from the craft store, make sure that this is made from strong plastic that has intricate designs so the finished product will come out beautifully after it comes out of the freezer.

Remember that this must never be washed using soap as this can mare the taste of the chocolate. You should simply use hot water and then dry it thoroughly using a dry cloth.

Each time you use the plastic mold, make sure to wipe it clean. Greasing, spraying or dusting is not needed as this will ruin the appearance of the finished candy.

But there is an exception to that rule. If you will be mixing your chocolate with some marshmallows, candy sprinkles, jellies or cooked candies, then you must first grease or spray the chocolate mold with oiling spray. This will make the chocolate easy to remove from the mold and if you are going to make another batch, the good news is that you only have to oil spray it once.

Next thing you need to learn is how to properly put

Homemade Chocolate: The Kickstart Guide on Making Delicious Chocolates

chocolate filling into the plastic sheet. For that, you use a regular teaspoon and fill each cavity with chocolate. Some of the chocolate might spill out but don't worry because you can clean that up later on.

There may be some air bubbles trapped within the chocolate. To release it, tap the filled mold on the counter to settle the chocolate. Another way is to hold the mold horizontally then gently drop it on the counter. You will probably have to do this several times until there all the air bubbles have been removed.

When the chocolate is ready, this is the time that you put this in the freezer. This is because it is the coolest place in the house taking it less time for the chocolate to harden so you can reuse the mold if you are making another batch of chocolates.

You will know when the chocolates are ready by looking at the back side of the mold. If the cavity appears to be graying, this means that the second you turn this over, the chocolate will easily fall off to the tray.

Homemade Chocolate: The Kickstart Guide on Making Delicious Chocolates

If it doesn't fall off on its own, you can tap it firmly. If this does not work, perhaps it needs a little more cooling time in the freezer so put it back in for a few minutes and then try again.

If you happen to have some leftovers from filling the mold, don't throw it away because you can use it again in the future. Just wait for the chocolate to harden so you can scrape it off and then wrap it in waxed paper.

You don't always need to make chocolate creations from molds even if this is the conventional way of doing it. The other option is to dip it in with other things like cookies or fruits so you have your own chocolate fondue as part of your dessert.

These days, you don't have to go to the grocery to buy chocolate. Just like cookies, these can be home made as long as you have the ingredients and the materials. They most important to make chocolate are the molds.

Molds are usually made of plastic and these can be purchased from craft stores. Most of these cost

Homemade Chocolate: The Kickstart Guide on Making Delicious Chocolates

about a dollar up so if you want to make these in different shapes and sizes, you have to buy a bunch.

Now that you have your mold, you should also buy the raw chocolate which is also available from the craft store. This is available in different flavors and colors so you can mix them up later on.

There are two ways to melt chocolate. The first is to cut the chocolate block into small pieces and then put this in a microwave safe bowl before sticking it in the oven. Since it is quite hard to see if all the chocolate has finally melted, we now come to the second option which is to melt it using a double boiler.

A double boiler consists of two pans. The first one has water while a smaller one is placed on top which is where the chocolate will be placed. You then stir the chocolate until melts. Once everything is now in liquid form, you then get your mold and pour the chocolate.

You should tap the bottom to take out air bubbles out of the chocolate otherwise there will be holes

Homemade Chocolate: The Kickstart Guide on Making Delicious Chocolates

later on when they come out of the freezer. If you decide to put in candy sprinkles or marshmallows with your chocolate, it is best to pour them into the boiler.

After ten minutes or so, the chocolate mold inside the freezer is ready to be taken out. A good indicator is to check the bottom of the mold and see if the chocolate is still holding on to the mold.

If it is ready, then it is time to flip it over and tap it gently so it can land on a soft surface like a napkin to prevent it from breaking. Another method is to carefully pour water on the mold. But if it is not, then you should put the mold back into the freezer.

The nice thing about working with chocolate is that if it should crack or break, you can recycle it which prevents wastage. If you make a mistake when you are painting it, don't touch it and wait until it freezes so it is easy to remove and you can start over.

When it is ready, you can serve this as part of your dessert but if you are giving this away as a

Homemade Chocolate: The Kickstart Guide on Making Delicious Chocolates

gift, make sure you find a nice box because it should look presentable to whoever will be receiving it.

Surely the molds you used to make chocolate will be used in the future. To maintain it, you must never wash this with soap as this removes its slickness. You should also carefully dry it after washing because it could cause spots to appear making it also difficult for the chocolate to be released from the mold.

But if your chocolate mold is sticky, perhaps you should coat it first lightly with some vegetable oil before you pour in the melted chocolate.

Making chocolate using molds is fun. You may not get it perfect the first time but as time goes by, you are sure to get better at it.

Chapter 10

Tips for Making Better Homemade Chocolate

Homemade Chocolate: The Kickstart Guide on Making Delicious Chocolates

When it comes to making homemade chocolates everyone has their own preferred methods that they use and really the only way to learn the best way to make homemade chocolate is to make some. But, here are some quick tips that you can use to make your homemade chocolate better that have been gathered over the years by expert chocolate makers and home chocolate makers alike. These tips can make your homemade chocolate creations even better:

•   When you buy chips or wafers of chocolate that you're going to melt as a chocolate base for your candy don't take them out of the plastic bags that they come in. Microwave them until they are melted or use a double boiler to melt them and then just cut a small hole in the corner of the bag and use the bag like a pastry bag to pour the chocolate into molds.

•   When you microwave chocolate to melt it start with just 1 minute and then keep microwaving it in 1 minute increments until it's melted. Every microwave is different and each type of chocolate has a different melting point so the time needed to melt the chocolate will be different on every microwave. Melting the chocolate in one minute increments means that you won't accidentally burn the chocolate.

• Don't freeze your chocolate concoctions. Freezing will start to make the chocolate break down and you'll lose the delicious flavor of homemade chocolate. Instead of freezing the chocolate store it in an airtight container at room temperature.

• Dark chocolate that is properly wrapped and stored will stay good for about a year, but milk chocolate will only stay good for about six months. If it's been longer than six months look for white spots on the chocolate. If the chocolate has white spots, called bloom, it means the chocolate is starting to separate and you should eat immediately or throw it out.

• To cut calories and make your homemade chocolate last longer take the homemade candy or chocolate bars that you made and cut them into a bunch of small pieces. Wrap the pieces and put them in the refrigerator. When you or the kids want a cold, sweet treat on a hot summer day take

Homemade Chocolate: The Kickstart Guide on Making Delicious Chocolates

out a piece of the cold homemade chocolate. It will have fewer calories and fat than ice cream or a full candy bar and will taste delicious.

• If you're really in a jam and you need some chocolate to finish making a batch of homemade chocolate and you're out of chocolate and don't have the time to run to the candy supply store or craft store and get more, or if the craft and hobby stores near you don't carry candy making chocolate you can get by with some melted chocolate chips. It's not a great solution, but it's a solution when you need some emergency chocolate for a recipe.

• If your chocolate does develop bloom and you are not going to eat it right away but don't want to throw it out you can melt the chocolate down, add some new ingredients, put it in new molds, and then wrap it and put it away.

Tips for Making Homemade Chocolates

Chocolate is used in a lot of desserts. These include ice cream, soufflés, custards and a host of other dishes. Almost everyone loves it because

Homemade Chocolate: The Kickstart Guide on Making Delicious Chocolates

studies have shown that it is an aphrodisiac. If you are too lazy to go to the store to buy one, why don't you make it yourself by following these tips.

First, you have to get ready all the materials and ingredients you will be using. The two most important happen to be the chocolate and the mold both which can be purchased at the craft store.

Chocolate comes in many flavors. Some examples of these are bitter sweet, milk, dark, semi-sweet, sweet and white. These are often sold in blocks if you don't have the time to convert these from cocoa beans. As for your molds, make sure that these are made from FDA approved food grade plastic.

You will also need sugar as this is a basic ingredient in most chocolates recipes. When you buy this from grocery, make sure that this does not have any trace of flour, salt or other kitchen ingredients.

Another important ingredient is unsalted butter. This is because the kind that contains salt is hard

Homemade Chocolate: The Kickstart Guide on Making Delicious Chocolates

to ascertain and there are instances where it could spoil the taste of your dish. You must never substitute butter with margarine if you don't have any because this will just make the cooking time longer as the water content here is much higher than that of butter.

There are three ways to liquefy chocolate before shaping this to its final form. You can heat this using the microwave, a double boiler or the oven. When making these into candies, it will be a good idea to also use a thermometer so you are able to monitor its temperature.

If you are using a thermometer that has a bulb, make sure that it does not touch the sides of the pan because this could give you the wrong reading.

When the chocolate is ready, this is the time that you put these into the mold. So it doesn't look messy, get some using a teaspoon and pour this into the cartridges. This is also the time you should add in other ingredients like peanuts, marshmallows or candy sprinkles.
If there are air bubbles, remove them by holding

Homemade Chocolate: The Kickstart Guide on Making Delicious Chocolates

the mold a few centimeters from the ground and dropping it on the table. You may have to do this several times to make sure that there is nothing left then you put these in the freezer.

You should check on your chocolate molds after 5 to 10 minutes. The bigger the mold, the longer it takes but you can check if it is ready by looking at the back of the mold. If a graying figure appears on the bottom, this means it is ready to be removed from the mold.

Once they are removed, put this in a plate or in a box if this is going to be given away. As for your molds, wash them in hot water and never with soap because this will remove its stickiness.

It should be dried thoroughly using a dry piece of cloth and stored properly so it looks good as new when you need to use it again.

You won't have any problems making homemade chocolates as long as you follow these tips. Who knows, this could open new doors for you like starting your own business.

Homemade Chocolate: The Kickstart Guide on Making Delicious Chocolates

Chapter 11

Tips for Packaging Your Homemade Chocolate

Homemade Chocolate: The Kickstart Guide on Making Delicious Chocolates

You can have a lot of fun packaging your homemade chocolate treats for a special occasion, to give as a gift, or just as a treat for the family or your friends. There are lots of different ways that you can package your homemade chocolate but when you're picking out packaging for your homemade chocolate one thing that you need to keep in mind is that the chocolate needs to be in something that is airtight if it's not going to be eaten immediately.

Because the first concern is always keeping the chocolate fresh usually homemade chocolate comes wrapped in two wrappers, one that is airtight and one that is decorative. You can choose a traditional gold colored candy box with pillow sheet inserts that are the same as other candy boxes. These are usually very similar to the boxes of candy that are popular as Valentine's Day and Christmas gifts.

Or you can use little cello bags that seal shut with a hair dryer or other heat source. Cello craft bags are easy to use and are very inexpensive. Often they come in different colors or prints so they are great for wrapping homemade chocolates as party

Homemade Chocolate: The Kickstart Guide on Making Delicious Chocolates

favors or birthday party treats. Cello bags can be found at any craft supply or candy supply store or if you are going to be using a lot of cello bags you can buy them in bulk online and get great discounts.

If you are making lollipops or suckers then cello bags are the best packaging to use because the cello bag won't stick to the chocolate like plastic wrap will. Put a cello bag over the top of the sucker, use a hair dryer to heat up the cello bag and the bag will mold to the shape of the candy without sticking to it. Put a ribbon or a sticker on the sucker and you have a sanitary package that will keep the chocolate fresh and looks cute.

The packaging that you use for your homemade chocolates is almost as important as the chocolate itself because the packaging is the finishing touch. Whatever type of packaging you pick for your homemade chocolate should be unique and should reflect your personality.

If you are making homemade chocolates for an event or a holiday using special theme packaging always makes a good impression. Even though

Homemade Chocolate: The Kickstart Guide on Making Delicious Chocolates

you might think it's not necessary to spend a lot of time or money on packaging your chocolate it's really worth it to take that last step and create a fun package for your chocolate.

After all, you worked hard to make a delicious treat, and in order to keep that treat delicious and safe to eat its necessary to put some kind of packaging on it. So pick out some wild or funk y packaging or even something sweet and traditional but make sure that whatever packaging you pick out expresses a little of your personality to make your chocolate really unique.

Creative packaging for your homemade chocolate doesn't have to be expensive to be great it just needs to be something that you designed yourself and put your own artistic stamp on.

Chapter 12

Homemade Chocolate Ideas for Christmas

Homemade Chocolate: The Kickstart Guide on Making Delicious Chocolates

Holidays are a great time to surprise your family and friends with homemade chocolates, and making homemade chocolate for Christmas is sure to make the holiday more festive. If you love to give personal gifts to your family and friends or if you are trying to keep your holidays spending budget low making homemade chocolates make great, inexpensive presents.

Here are some ideas that you can use to make your Christmas holiday more festive with homemade chocolate.

•   Homemade chocolates that are wrapped in plastic and then arranged in a pretty holiday tin make wonderful inexpensive gifts for teachers, ministers, postal carriers, newspaper carriers, delivery people, bosses, Secret Santa gift exchanges and holiday parties.

•   When you need to bring a dessert to a holiday party and you want your dessert to really stand out make some homemade chocolates and arrange them on a holiday serving platter with a fresh fruit garnish.

Homemade Chocolate: The Kickstart Guide on Making Delicious Chocolates

• Homemade chocolates make great stocking stuffers.

• Use some of your homemade chocolate to make some rich holiday hot chocolate to enjoy on a cold winter night.

• Need gifts for a large amount of people, like all the people in your office, or each of the 30 kids in your child's class at school? Put one or two homemade chocolates in a small candy box and have your child decorate the outside of the box with markers, glue and paint and you have a unique gift that doesn't cost a lot or take a lot of time to make.

• Use your holiday cookie cutters to cut out some homemade chocolate fudge in holiday shapes.

• Make sugar free and low fat homemade chocolates instead of Christmas cookies to try and keep the amount of holiday calories that you eat under control.

• Make some homemade chocolate bar or chocolate cherry bark and arrange it on a platter

Homemade Chocolate: The Kickstart Guide on Making Delicious Chocolates

with some fresh fruit and use that as an edible centerpiece for your holiday table.

Chapter 13

Making the Holidays More Festive with Homemade Chocolate Drinks

Homemade Chocolate: The Kickstart Guide on Making Delicious Chocolates

Almost everyone loves hot chocolate, and during the winter holidays hot chocolate drinks are everywhere. Hot chocolate is a great drink to have at parties where people might not want to drink alcohol and where kids will be present. Homemade hot chocolate mixes also make great gifts.

So this year instead of spending a lot of money on fancy hot chocolate mixes to give as gifts or to keep in the pantry for family and friends you should make your own unique hot chocolate mixes that you use to serve hot chocolate to guests or use as gifts and stocking stuffers.

Homemade hot chocolate mixes are easy to make. The first thing that you need to make homemade hot chocolate is cocoa powder. You can buy sweetened or unsweetened cocoa powder in the grocery store; it's usually in the aisle where the chocolate milk powders and syrups are kept.

Then you need some powdered non dairy creamer or powdered milk. Creamer will make your homemade hot chocolate very rich so most

Homemade Chocolate: The Kickstart Guide on Making Delicious Chocolates

experts suggest that you use mostly powdered milk but add a touch of powdered creamer just to add a little richness to your hot chocolate mix. Use a flavored non dairy creamer to enhance the flavor of the hot cocoa.

Once you have a cocoa powder and milk or creamer base you can use your imagination and cooking skills to put together some exotic hot cocoa mix treats.

Here are some fun ideas that you can use to make your own tasty hot chocolate this holiday season:

• For people that are diabetic or can't have sugar use unsweetened cocoa and use a sugar substitute to sweeten the cocoa powder.

• Add spices and herbs to make Mexican hot chocolate or other types of hot and spicy hot chocolate.

• Add dried fruit and herbs to give your hot chocolate a kick.

Homemade Chocolate: The Kickstart Guide on Making Delicious Chocolates

•   Add mini marshmallows to make a hot chocolate mix everyone will love.

•   Combine different types of cocoa powder to get different flavors.

•   To make low fat hot chocolate mix use dark cocoa powder and low fat creamer and milk.

•   To make a very personal gift on a budget make up several different kinds of hot chocolate mixes and package them in plastic bags that are inside pretty envelopes and pack them in a basket with two mugs and some homemade chocolates or cookies.

When you're packaging your hot chocolate it's a good idea to list all the ingredients on the package in case someone that you are giving the hot chocolate too is allergic to one of the ingredients.

Chapter 14

Homemade Chocolate Ideas for Easter

Homemade Chocolate: The Kickstart Guide on Making Delicious Chocolates

Every chocolate lover gets excited around Easter because no Easter celebration would be complete without lots of chocolate. You can make the Easter holiday much more personal and save a lot of money on Easter baskets if you make your own homemade chocolate treats for Easter.

Since nearly everyone goes overboard and eats too much chocolate during the Easter holiday it's a good idea to make low calorie, low fat, or sugar free chocolate during Easter. That way you can eat the same amount of candy but you'll be eating fewer calories and less fat, and so will your kids.

Here are some ideas that you can use to make your own homemade chocolates for Easter:

•   Put your own twist on classic chocolate bunnies by using exotic chocolates or an unusual chocolate base like chocolate mixed with spices or fruit to make chocolate bunnies.

•   Make edible homemade chocolate baskets instead of chocolate bunnies, then arrange other holiday treats inside the basket. To make a chocolate Easter basket melt some base

Homemade Chocolate: The Kickstart Guide on Making Delicious Chocolates

chocolate in a plastic bag and blow up a small balloon. Put the balloon inside the bag of melted chocolate until the bottom half of the balloon is thickly coated with chocolate and then immediately move the balloon to the refrigerator.

•   Once the chocolate hardens pop the balloon and pull the balloon out and you'll have a solid chocolate Easter basket that you can use for your kids or as a holiday table centerpiece. You can even use white chocolate as a base and dye it with food coloring to make your chocolate baskets in different colors. Be careful though! The chocolate will melt if left out in the warm weather.

•   If you want to cut down on the amount of sugar that your kids will be eating during the Easter holiday make a chocolate dipping sauce and then cut fruit into Easter shapes and dip the fruit into the chocolate. Once the chocolate hardens your kids will have a sweet holiday treat with a lot less sugar and calories.

•   Instead of decorating hard boiled eggs in pretty colors make some dark chocolate eggs and use candy coloring to pain the chocolate eggs the way that you would paint traditional hard boiled eggs.

• Most Easter candies are made from milk chocolate so stay away from using milk chocolate in your homemade Easter candy bases and use something more exotic to make your homemade chocolate stand out more.

Chapter 15

Homemade Chocolate Ideas for Other Holidays

Homemade Chocolate: The Kickstart Guide on Making Delicious Chocolates

You can make a lot of great gifts, party favors, centerpieces and other for other holidays too. Here are some fun ways to use homemade chocolates for other holidays:

For Valentine's Day

Nothing says "I love you" like some homemade chocolates on Valentine's Day. Since the price of candy and flowers usually goes sky high around Valentine's Day making your own homemade chocolates for your sweetheart can be a great way to save money and still give that special someone a gift that they'll love. When you need a special homemade valentine treat you can:

•   Make homemade chocolates using some "naughty" chocolate molds for a little bit of fun.

•   Plan a sensuous dessert by cutting up some fresh fruit and making an exotic, spicy chocolate dipping sauce.

•   Make your sweetie a dozen chocolate rose lollipops instead of giving a dozen roses.

Homemade Chocolate: The Kickstart Guide on Making Delicious Chocolates

• Use Valentine themed cookie cutters to make special chocolate bars and fudge pieces.

• Make homemade chocolates that your child can bring to school and share with classmates instead of buying expensive valentines.

• Surprise your sweetie with heart shaped pancakes and homemade chocolate sauce for breakfast.

• Make some special hot chocolate mixes as gifts for friends and family.

• Mix up an exotic chocolate sauce and serve it warm over some cold ice cream.

• Have an Anti- Valentine's Day party and make some dark chocolate broken heart candies for your friends that are single.

• Make homemade chocolate gift bags for everyone in the office.

• Use Valentine's Day molds to create chocolate Cupids and then decorate them with

71

Homemade Chocolate: The Kickstart Guide on Making Delicious Chocolates

candy coloring. Give one to everyone you meet on Valentine's Day.

•　　Make yourself a special Valentine's Day chocolate treat and fill some dark chocolate truffles with champagne and a little rosewater.

•　　Make a box of homemade chocolates for your partner and top each one with a rose petal.

For Mother's Day

Mother's Day is another holiday that you can make a lot more special by giving homemade chocolate. Remember when you were little and your mom loved the presents that you made with your own hands the best? Moms always love handmade presents the best, so this year make her some delicious homemade chocolate treats. The only limit to making homemade chocolate gifts is your imagination, but here are some ideas to get you started:

•　　Use a soap mold of a mother and child in a cameo to make some special Mother's Day chocolates. Make sure that you use a chocolate

Homemade Chocolate: The Kickstart Guide on Making Delicious Chocolates

base that is made up of mom's favorite types of chocolate.

•	Make a gift basket for mom that has homemade chocolates, special hot chocolate mixes, new mugs, and a soothing CD to play when she needs to relax.

•	Make coupons that promise your mother a homemade chocolate treat every month, along with a visit from you.

•	Sit down and share a cup of tea and some homemade chocolate with your mom.

•	Make a sauce of mom's favorite chocolate and drizzle it over some buttered popcorn to make chocolate pop corn balls. Mom will love to have a crunchy, sweet snack to enjoy when she's watching TV.

•	Start Mother's Day off with a special breakfast of chocolate covered fruit.

•	If you have small children making homemade chocolate is a fantastic way for the

Homemade Chocolate: The Kickstart Guide on Making Delicious Chocolates

kids to make something to give to their mom, but always supervise them when they're around the hot liquid chocolate.

•   Have your kids decorate gift boxes with glitter and crayons and pack the boxes full of homemade chocolates.

•   Have each child make a handprint in chocolate for mom.

•   Give your mom the best gift you can give her, the gift of your time. Spend the afternoon in the kitchen with your mom making homemade chocolate together and eating everything that you make.

Handmade gifts mean more to mothers than probably anyone else, and making some homemade chocolate to give to your mom is a gift that she'll remember so this year instead of buying her another robe or taking her to a fancy brunch that is crowded and overpriced just make her some homemade chocolate and watch her face light up.

Chapter 16

Homemade Chocolate Ideas for Birthdays

Homemade Chocolate: The Kickstart Guide on Making Delicious Chocolates

Birthday parties and homemade chocolate go hand in hand. There are a lot of ways that you can use homemade chocolate at birthday parties as an inexpensive, easy to make party favor. Homemade chocolate is always a big hit but homemade chocolate goes over especially well at kids' birthday parties. Here are some fun ways that you can use homemade chocolate to liven up birthday parties.

•   Make homemade chocolate lollipops for your kid's birthday party. Lollipops and chocolate suckers are great party favors because they can be individually wrapped and they are easy to carry around. Even if your child's birthday party is somewhere else like a restaurant or park or museum you can easily hand out homemade chocolate suckers as party favors.

•   Make sugar free homemade chocolates in shapes that fit with the theme of the party. Get a bulk order or small Chinese food take out boxes, the little white boxes with wire handles to put the chocolates in. You can get them in bulk online. Put out crayons, stickers, glitter, glue and other materials and let the kids decorate their own party

Homemade Chocolate: The Kickstart Guide on Making Delicious Chocolates

favor box then fill the boxes with homemade sugar free chocolate as the kids are leaving. The other parents will appreciate that the candies are sugar free and the kids will have a sweet treat to take home.

•   Make chocolate boxes for the kids to put their other party favors into and take home. Chocolate boxes are always a smash at birthday parties. You can make chocolate boxes for grownup birthday parties too, and put grownup party favors in them. Homemade chocolate boxes are always a favorite party favor.

•   If the kids are old enough make one of the party activities making their own chocolate. You can melt the chocolate in the microwave for them but then let them add their own fun items into the chocolate like nuts, candy, fruit and so on and let them choose a mold, pour their chocolate concoction in it and by the time the party is over the chocolate should be hard and ready to take home.

•   For grownup parties, set up a chocolate fountain flowing with some delicious homemade chocolate sauce and set up a fruit bar full of fresh

Homemade Chocolate: The Kickstart Guide on Making Delicious Chocolates

fruit for dipping. This gives people that are concerned about their calorie intake a low calorie dessert alternative to birthday cake.

•   Use homemade chocolates as the prizes for some of the party games and let each winner choose their own gift bag full of delicious chocolates.

•   At grownup parties give out a mug with a decorated packet of special hot chocolate mix inside and print the recipe on the envelope so your guests can make it at home.

It's almost a must that you serve something chocolate at birthday parties. If you are the kind of person that doesn't really care for chocolate then you can serve some homemade chocolate for your guests so that they will have some chocolate to enjoy.

Chapter 17

Homemade Chocolate Ideas for
Weddings and Wedding Showers

Homemade Chocolate: The Kickstart Guide on Making Delicious Chocolates

You might not have thought about using homemade chocolates as wedding or wedding shower favors but homemade chocolates fit in perfectly at weddings and wedding showers. Homemade chocolate wedding favors are also a great way for the bride and groom to save some money because homemade wedding favors will cost a lot less than commercial ones.

At a wedding you give you favors to your friends and family to thank them for coming to celebrate the wedding with you. Since homemade chocolates are a very personal and individual gift they are the perfect "thank you" for friends and family. There are hundreds of ways that you can incorporate homemade chocolates into your wedding but here are just a few of the most popular ways that people use homemade chocolates as wedding favors:

• Get some plastic champagne glasses and fill them with individually wrapped homemade chocolates. Place a square of tulle over the top and tie the tulle down with a ribbon so that the chocolates don't fall out. Place one at each guest's seat.

Homemade Chocolate: The Kickstart Guide on Making Delicious Chocolates

•   Chocolate boxes made in the shape of a heart with the bride and groom's names and the date carved into them are elegant party favors that are a big hit with guests. If you want to make them even more personal carve each guest's name into a chocolate box, just make sure that you give the right box to the right guest!

•   Bottles of chocolate dipping sauce labeled with the bride and groom's name and the dates and a kitchy name are fun wedding favors.

•   Give your guests packets of special hot chocolate and two mugs in a basket with a book of love poems and instructions for them to sit and read the book together over a cup of special homemade hot chocolate.

•   Make a centerpiece of homemade chocolate roses on sticks that are decorated to look like stems and have each guest take one of the chocolate roses home with them at the end of the night.

•   In the kid's area set up a station where kids can make their own chocolate to keep them

Homemade Chocolate: The Kickstart Guide on Making Delicious Chocolates

occupied. Just make that they are supervised and that aprons are available to protect their nice clothes.

•　　Have a chocolate fountain flowing with a special "signature" chocolate flavor and have plenty of strawberries and other fresh fruit available for dipping.

•　　A great wedding favor is to package a few homemade chocolates with a small, handwritten recipe book full of great recipes for homemade chocolates. Give the recipes fun names like "Spice up your marriage Spicy Hot Chocolate".

Homemade Chocolate Ideas for Wedding Showers

Homemade chocolates are the perfect party favors for wedding showers. Most women love chocolate, and love handmade things, so giving your friends and family some special chocolates made just for them as a way of saying "thank you" to them for coming to celebrate your impending marriage is a lovely way to let them know you appreciate them. Here are some fun ideas that

Homemade Chocolate: The Kickstart Guide on Making Delicious Chocolates

you can use to make handmade chocolate wedding shower favors for your friends and family:

• If you are having an "adult" wedding shower then some homemade chocolates in adult shapes are a lot of fun and a great conversation piece.

• One of the most popular wedding shower favors is a small box of homemade truffles or other fancy chocolates tied with a bow. Usually the box and ribbon are in the bride's wedding colors. If you want to make the favors extra special take a moment to write a personal message on each box.

• Chocolate boxes are also fun for wedding showers, especially when they are filled with other small gifts.

• Small chocolate bars imprinted with the bride's name or a cute saying and wrapped in individualized packaging are inexpensive and cute wedding shower favors if you have a lot of guests attending the shower.

• Since there are lots of women that watch their weight very carefully a low calorie chocolate dipping sauce and some fresh fruit is a nice alternative dessert at a wedding shower for women that don't want to indulge in cake or other high calorie desserts.

• A handmade chocolate dipping sauce in a personalized bottle makes a nice wedding shower favor. Make sure that you have a few sugar free bottles for anyone that needs to have sugar free chocolate.

• You can also serve a "cake" made up entirely of small boxes of individual homemade chocolates and decorated with ribbons in the bride's colors. Arrange the boxes on a cake platter to look like a layer cake and you'll have a beautiful alternative to a high calorie cake that is already portioned out.

• If you want to celebrate your friendship with the friends and family who have attended the shower a nice party favor is a special mug that contains a packet of homemade hot chocolate mix and a coupon for one afternoon chat with you where you can share the hot chocolate.

• Need a special wedding shower favor for

Homemade Chocolate: The Kickstart Guide on Making Delicious Chocolates

your maid of honor? Pack a gift basket full of homemade chocolates, chocolate covered popcorn, two DVDs of movies that you always watch together and a cozy throw blanket so that the two of you can get together, watch movies, and share some homemade chocolates before you get married.

Chapter 18

Homemade Chocolate Ideas for Other Occasions

Homemade Chocolate: The Kickstart Guide on Making Delicious Chocolates

You don't need a holiday or a wedding or a birthday as an excuse to make some homemade chocolate. Homemade chocolates are always a treat, and almost any party or gathering is more fun with some homemade chocolate.

Whether you are looking for an activity to keep the kids busy on a rainy afternoon, or a project that you and your child can do together, or something special that you can make for a friend on a limited budget spending a little time and a little money making homemade chocolate can really brighten your day, or your someone else's.

Here are some easy and inexpensive ways that you can use homemade chocolates to brighten someone's day:

• If you have been very busy lately and haven't had a lot of time leftover to do things with your kids make a date to spend just an hour in the evening making homemade chocolates with them. The process of making chocolate is easy and fun and it will give you a chance to reconnect with your kids.

Homemade Chocolate: The Kickstart Guide on Making Delicious Chocolates

•   Make some homemade chocolates in heart shapes after your spouse goes to bed and leave a small box of homemade candy tied with a red ribbon on his/her pillow the next morning.

•   Surprise a co-worker that has been having a hard time adjusting to something at work with a "pick me up" gift box of homemade chocolates and some special tea and a mug.

•   Leave some special homemade hot chocolate mixes in the break room at work so that everyone can enjoy a nice sweet treat in the afternoon.

•   Send a small box of homemade chocolates in fun shapes to school with your kids for their teachers as a small "thank you" gift for no reason.

•   When one of your friends has a bad breakup or has relationship problems leave a gift basket on her doorstep with some homemade chocolates, a DVD of her favorite movie, some wine, and new silk pajamas or a cozy bathrobe and slippers.

Homemade Chocolate: The Kickstart Guide on Making Delicious Chocolates

•   Put some small, individually wrapped pieces of homemade chocolate in your child's jacket pocket at random times.

•   When you leave a tip for the waiter at your favorite restaurant or the barista that makes your coffee leave a few individually wrapped homemade chocolates too.

•   Bring over some homemade hot chocolate and two mugs to a lonely neighbor, then sit down and talk and share the hot chocolate.

Chapter 19

Making Gourmet Homemade Chocolate

Homemade Chocolate: The Kickstart Guide on Making Delicious Chocolates

Most of the time when people think about making homemade chocolate they think about someone working in the kitchen and making some chocolate that is tasty, but not really the kind of high end chocolate that you find in a gourmet store somewhere. But you can make gourmet chocolate at home, and it doesn't have to cost a fortune to make.

If you have a very sophisticated palette and you really enjoy gourmet chocolate but don't like paying $7 or more for a gourmet chocolate bar you can easily make your own gourmet chocolate at home.

The ingredients make the chocolate. Whenever you are baking or cooking the quality of the ingredients that you use really make a difference. If you bake cookies with butter instead of margarine you can taste the difference. If you use real vanilla extract instead of imitation vanilla you will taste the different. The same principle applies when you're making gourmet chocolate at home. Using only high quality ingredients is a must if you want to make the kind of chocolate that your friends and family will swear you bought from a

Homemade Chocolate: The Kickstart Guide on Making Delicious Chocolates

gourmet shop.

If you want to make gourmet chocolate but you don't want to go to the extreme of ordering cacao beans, roasting them, grinding them, and going through the entire traditional candy making process you can buy melt and pour style chocolate bases that are made from higher end ingredients that most of the melt and pour style chocolate but you will need to get those from a specialty candy store not the local craft and hobby store.

Online there are several retailers that specialize in selling high end gourmet chocolate making materials to homemade chocolate makers. An online search should turn up a few shops that you can order high quality melt and pour style chocolate from. Another ingredient that is really important when you're making gourmet chocolate is the add-ins that you're putting in your chocolate.

The trick to saving money on your add-ins is to hit up your local farmer's market or grocery co-op to get the best organic ingredients at decent prices. You can buy organic nuts, make your own peanut

Homemade Chocolate: The Kickstart Guide on Making Delicious Chocolates

butter blends, get special organic and luxury syrups and sugars and oils and fresh herbs like lavender and rosehips to add into your gourmet chocolate.

When you're making gourmet chocolate you can also add in different kinds of high end alcohol to some of your chocolate to give it a great exotic taste. For example you could pair a high quality dark chocolate base with some raspberry flavored vodka and a few dried raspberries to make a wonderfully dark and sweet homemade chocolate. Or you could add some high end cognac to a gourmet chocolate dipping sauce that you would use to dip fruit into.

Making gourmet chocolate might take more practice than making regular homemade chocolate because the flavors in gourmet chocolate need to be very subtle but if you love gourmet chocolate you can learn to make it at home and have a lot of fun making your own gourmet chocolate flavors.

Chapter 20

Making Money Selling Homemade Chocolate

Homemade Chocolate: The Kickstart Guide on Making Delicious Chocolates

Once you have discovered the joys of making homemade chocolate and you have caused your friends and family to gain weight with your constant gifts of homemade chocolate you might discover that you have a real passion for making homemade chocolate. If you are truly passionate about making homemade chocolate and you want to try and make a little extra money you could try selling your homemade chocolate.

The first thing that you need to do if you want to start selling your homemade chocolate is to find out what the licensing requirements are in your state to have a commercial kitchen and you will need to either have your kitchen inspected or rent a kitchen that has been inspected. Once you have a certificate saying that your kitchen is approved so you will be ready to start making homemade chocolate for sale.

Once you have the necessary paperwork to start selling homemade chocolate you'll have to figure out what your niche market is. Who are you trying to sell homemade chocolates to? Are you going to make homemade chocolate wedding favors and other party favors or are you going to focus on

Homemade Chocolate: The Kickstart Guide on Making Delicious Chocolates

making homemade chocolates for gifts or do you want to do it all and just make as many types of homemade chocolate as you can?

Sometimes people get started selling their homemade chocolates by selling them at craft fairs, church sales and other places where they are already known to most of the people that are attending. Getting family and friends to buy your homemade chocolate can be a great way to start a small side business selling your homemade chocolate.

If you decide to start selling your homemade chocolate then it's a good idea to sit down and map out a basis business plan and set some goals for your business. Even if you just want to sell your homemade chocolate part time on the side it helps to have a business plan and some idea of what your expenses for the business are.

Once you're ready to start taking orders you can set up a website where people can order homemade chocolates from you. Make sure that you do some research into the different types of shipping methods available and how much each

Homemade Chocolate: The Kickstart Guide on Making Delicious Chocolates

one costs because each freight carrier will have their own set of rules about shipping food.

If you don't want to bother with the hassles of shipping food you can also sell wholesale to local stores and bakeries. If you are making gourmet chocolate at home then local gourmet stores or your local food co-op might be interested in buying your locally produced homemade chocolate in bulk to sell in their stores. Local stores will also sometimes accept consignment sales where you pay them a percentage of what you make.

If you really love making homemade chocolate and you have developed a lot of your own special and unique recipes and you love coming up with new recipes then you might also want to think about selling homemade chocolate recipe books or starting a blog about your passion for homemade chocolate making.

Homemade chocolate making can be a great hobby, and it can make you some extra money too if you are willing to put the time and effort into making your business grow.

Homemade Chocolate: The Kickstart Guide on Making Delicious Chocolates

Conclusion

Homemade Chocolate: The Kickstart Guide on Making Delicious Chocolates

Hopefully you have gotten a lot of ideas and learned a lot about making chocolate at home through the course of this book. Making chocolate at home is a fun, exciting hobby that can be a great way to show your friends and family how much they mean to you. Nothing tells someone you love them quite like giving them a homemade gift, and an edible gift like homemade chocolate is always appreciated.

Making homemade chocolate can also save you a lot of money on gifts. Birthday gifts, holiday gifts, anniversary gifts and other gifts can get quite pricey and if you have a lot of friends and family then you probably almost always have to buy an expensive gift for someone. Making homemade chocolate can be a lot less expensive than buying gifts and it gives you a chance to make something really unique.

Making your own homemade chocolate can also be a way for you to get to spend more time with your kids. Parents that work and are very busy often don't get to spend a lot of quality time with their children and making some homemade chocolate together can be a nice chance to

Homemade Chocolate: The Kickstart Guide on Making Delicious Chocolates

connect with your children and talk about how they are doing while you make a tasty treat that you can enjoy together.

If you love to cook and you love making homemade chocolate and you eventually want to open your own small business making homemade chocolate being creative and finding fun ways to use homemade chocolate will be the keys to your success. The ideas and tips in this book should help you get started on that journey.

Good luck to you as you dive into the exciting world of making homemade chocolate!

Homemade Chocolate: The Kickstart Guide on Making Delicious Chocolates

Recommended Resources

Homemade Chocolate: The Kickstart Guide on Making Delicious Chocolates

Books:

Truffles: 50 Deliciously Decadent Homemade Chocolate Treats (50 Series) by Dede Wilson

Chocolates and Confections at Home with The Culinary Institute of America by Peter Greweling

Blissfully Chocolate - Classic Cake, Biscuit and Dessert Recipes (Ambrosial Delights From the Past) by Maggie David

Websites:

http://www.wikihow.com/Make-Chocolate

http://www.makingchocolatecandytips.com/how-to-make-homemade-chocolates

http://www.ehow.com/how_2041142_make-homemade-chocolate.html

About the Author

Lynne Parcell is an accomplished writer who enjoys researching and writing on a variety of subjects. For more information and the newest Kickstart Guide releases, visit the author page at:

http://KickstartGuidesOnline.com

2154092R00060

Printed in Great Britain
by Amazon.co.uk, Ltd.,
Marston Gate.